The CLOUD and I

Pictures and Story by: *Mary Ann Kratzer*

To order additional copies of this book, contact:
Xlibris
1-888-795-4274
www.Xlibris.com
Orders@Xlibris.com

Pictures and Story by: Mary Ann Kratzer

As I was lying in the grass
One bright and sunny day,
I looked up to the sky and watched
some small white clouds at play.

The sun cast down its golden rays
and sprinkled them around.
They touched the edges of the clouds
then dropped down to the ground.

What is it like to be a cloud?
I wondered to myself;
When suddenly one drifted down,
It looked just like an elf!

It said to me, "Hello my friend,"
And puffed up very proud;
"I'm here to help you find out what
it's like to be a cloud."

It took my hand and whisked me off
high up into the sky.
We saw some birds and an airplane,
and waved as they passed by.

It said, "We're tiny drops of water
suspended in the air.
We're different shapes and sizes
And can travel anywhere."

It took me to the land of clouds
and introduced me to,
Nimbus, Stratus, and Cumulus,
just to name a few.

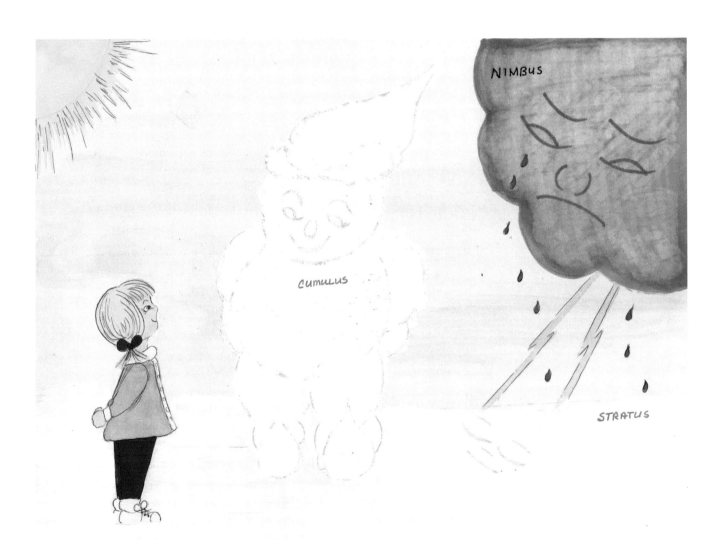

"Nimbus is the grumpy one,
it's colored black and grey;
It spreads for miles across the sky
but quickly moves away."

"Sometimes it has a temper fit
and thunders loud and long.
It flashes lightening to the ground,
It's winds are swift and strong."

"Stratus is the lazy cloud
and lowest to the ground,
It stretches out so long and flat
and never makes a sound."

"It's such a boring, sleepy cloud
that seldom changes shape,
It's happy just to float along
in a slow and dreamy state."

"The only one left to tell you about is
the happy white cumulus cloud.
Since I am part of this billowy group,
you'll know why I am so proud."

"We tumble and roll all over the sky
and pile on top of each other,
We look like mountains of marshmallow pies
or mashed potatoes in butter."

"We like to play make believe games
and change into things we are not
Like kangaroos and elephants too,
or pigs with very large snouts."

"Look at me, I think I can be a mouse,
just one of a kind.
Oh me, Oh my, what have I done?
I've left my long tail behind."

It was ready to leave, my special friend,
and spiraled like smoke to the sky.
"I hope you enjoyed this wonderful day,
but now, I must say goodbye."

When I grow up and am flying around
in an airplane high in the sky,
I hope to see my friend, the cloud,
from inside a big marshmallow pie.

Printed in the United States
By Bookmasters